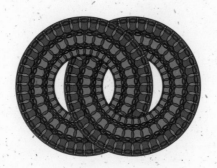

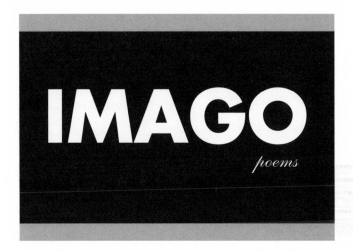

IMAGO

poems

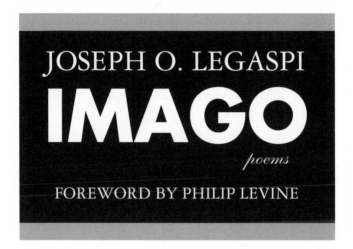

JOSEPH O. LEGASPI

IMAGO

poems

FOREWORD BY PHILIP LEVINE

CavanKerry ❖ Press LTD.

CavanKerry Press Ltd.
Fort Lee, New Jersey
www.cavankerrypress.org

Library of Congress Cataloging-in-Publication Data

Legaspi, Joseph O., 1971–
Imago : poems / Joseph O. Legaspi. — 1st ed.
p. cm.
ISBN-13: 978-1-933880-03-7
ISBN-10: 1-933880-03-1
I. Title.

PS3612.E3514I43 2007
811'.6--dc22

2007014094

Cover art, *The Compensatory Motif in the Libidinal Economy of a Painter's
Bad Inconscience*, by Manuel Ocampo © 2006
Author photograph by Emmy Catedral
Cover and book design by Peter Cusack

First Edition 2007
Printed in the United States of America

NEW✧VOICES

CavanKerry Press is dedicated to springboarding the careers of previously unpublished poets by bringing to print two to three New Voices annually. Manuscripts are selected from open submission; CavanKerry Press does not conduct competitions or charge reading fees.

CavanKerry Press is grateful for the support it receives from the New Jersey State Council on the Arts.

Acknowledgements

Many thanks to the editors of the following publications, in which many of the poems in this collection—or varying manifestations of them—first appeared: *Asian Pacific American Journal, Babaylan, Bamboo Ridge, Bloomsbury Review, Blue Mesa Review, Chaminade Literary Review, Coe Review, Crab Orchard Review, DisOrient, The Drunken Boat, Flyway, Gulf Coast, Hayden's Ferry Review, Hyphen, La Petite Zine, The Ledge, The Literary Review, Many Mountains Moving, MiPOesias, Mudfish, North American Review, Our Own Voice, Poet Lore, Puerto Del Sol, Second Avenue, Seneca Review, Sou'Wester, S.P.A.W.N.,* and *Spoon River Poetry Review.*

"The Immigrants' Son," "This Face," "Killing a Chicken," and "The Mother" (from "Three Muses") appeared in the anthology *Tilting the Continent: Southeast Asian American Writing*, edited by Shirley Geok-lin Lim and Cheng Lok Chua (New Rivers Press, 2000).

"Imago" and "The Circumcision" appeared in the anthology *PinoyPoetics*, edited by Nick Carbó (Meritage Press, 2004).

"Ode to My Mother's Hair" appeared in the anthology *Contemporary Voices of the Eastern World: An Anthology of Poems*, edited by Tina Chang, Nathalie Handal, and Ravi Shankar (W.W. Norton, 2007).

§§§

Heartfelt gratitude to my poetry professors throughout the years: Galway Kinnell, Sharon Olds, the late William Matthews, Gail Wronsky, and Philip Levine.

To Sarah Gambito, my partner in crime, my Grace: a delectable cauldron of the creamiest mac&cheese, with bacon, the food of joy.

Spot o' tea & treacle pudding with warm custard to the following for their [relentless] friendships, pimpin' &/or poetic feedback/assistance/inspiration: Kron Vollmer, Patrick Rosal, Jennifer Chang, Vikas Menon, January

Gill O' Neil, PJ Harvey, Oliver de la Paz, Aimee Nezhukumatathil, Jon Pineda, Kundiman, FireCircle (Rita Zilberman, Kathleen Andersen, Saladin Ahmed . . .), Kate Bush, The Pulitzer Prizes, Barbara Alaniz, Natalie "Scout" Sullaway, Sergio Marin, Tori Amos, Kaliko Kauahi, Manuel Ocampo, Bud Shark, Eddie del Rosario, Emmy Catedral, Belle & Sebastian, Mariko Nagai, David Simpson, Soo Jin Oh, Caitlin Grace McDonnell, Corinne Domingo, Harper Lee, Baron Wormser, Marilyn Chin, Lawson Inada, Arthur Sze, Paolo Javier, Sanjana Nair, my beloved New York City, &, not in the least, in loving memory, Phebus Etienne.

Finally, love & respect to my family—immediate & extended—& their stories.

To my Mother & Father,
my reluctant muses

§§§

In memory of Rosario Gardner Orense (1917 ~ 2006)

ima·go

Pronunciation: i-'mä-(")gO, -'mA-

Function: *noun*

Inflected Form(s): *plural* **imagoes** or **ima·gi·nes** (-gə-nẽz)

Etymology: New Latin, from Latin, image

1 : an insect in its final, adult, sexually mature, and typically winged state after metamorphosis.

2 : an idealized mental image of the self or another person usually a parent, formed in childhood and persisting unconsciously into adulthood.

(—From *The American Heritage Dictionary of the English Language*, 4th ed.)

Contents

Foreword

There are those who regret that American poetry no longer resembles the poems they memorized back in the ninth grade, the ones that celebrated battles and snowdrifts. You can still encounter such folks at colloquies of high school teachers of physical education and among those who gather at conventions of dead languages to lament the passing of the great age of prosody which accompanied our dismal fifties. Fortunately there are fewer and fewer of them each year. The dominant American poetic DNA still belongs to Walt Whitman though most of those who attempt poetry in this country also carry a recessive gene of Ms. Dickinson to keep them honest. In truth the open house of American poetry contains a well-rounded family, and if it had a motto on its doorstep it would more likely resemble "Enter and be recognized" rather than "Abandon hope, all ye who enter here."

Which brings me to the present collection of poetry, one that might not have found a home in the restrictive poetry publishing world of sixty years ago, but today a collection as original and startling as this one is a necessary part of the multicolored kaleidoscope we call American literature. Its author, Joseph O. Legaspi, now of New York City, was born and raised in the Philippines, and of course his work reflects that heritage, not only reflects it but weds it to the American experience. You might regard the work as exotic, but if you did you'd have to regard half the poetry written in our country today as exotic.

The first three sections of the book are set in the landscape of childhood, a childhood probably quite different from your own, but with two familiar dominant figures: the creative, charismatic, powerful father and the tender, nurturing mother. The poems are portraits of village life in what resembles a preindustrial world without telephones, air conditioners, even printed books, almost—one is tempted to say—without evil. The bonds of familial and brotherly love are lasting and fierce. It is a kind of primal Eden in which at first everyone seems innocent.

> My mermaid, I watched you scaling milkfish.
> Your hands and arms were silver,
> and your body flecked
> with otherworldly raindrops.

You were a silver mine to be mined.

(From "Imagined Love Poems to My Mother from My Father")

Not many poets could find singular love and beauty in such a brutal and necessary chore as gutting and scaling fish. Or from the poem "The Bringers of Bread" this passage which evokes the magic of childhood to a degree astonishing in the new poetry of this century:

At the bakery, we bask in the clean scent
of newly baked *pan de sal*, providers that we are.
We press the brown bags to our hunter's
breasts and let the warmth seep beneath our ribs.

Within a few pages we know we are reading an adult, and we soon discover that even in this boy's world of innocent adventures and the safety of a totally fixed and ritualized existence the threat of sex, pain, and death are present as is also the knowledge that sooner or later we will all bow to them. In the poem "The Sow" "a tusked boar the color of smudged mud" is helped by breeders to mount the family's pink sow tied to a post. As she shrieks the boy narrator of the poem imagines "her backbone breaking at any second."

Soon there will be piglets, too.
To feed and to sell.
We watch as the sow bends her front knees,
her wail as much a part of us as the morning air.

Legaspi, like William Carlos Williams, can find poetry anywhere. And like his mentor Pablo Neruda he seems able to locate the mysterious and the magical in the most common and overlooked objects. His little poem "The Socks" is the most amazing poem on that subject I have encountered since Neruda's great ode on the same subject, and while paying tribute to his Chilean master Legaspi takes the poem in an entirely different direction. It ends:

When I slip into them,

I see my father in his footwear, like Mercury,
a copper-eyed young man, like myself,

brewing with stormy promise,
prepared to soar above the dusty world.

Dear socks, don't lead me astray.
Propel me from this dissatisfied life

to places where my father has never been.

The fourth and final section of the book depicts the departure from childhood and the family's island life for a meaner existence here in the United States. Once mother and father were queen and king, but now she works twenty hours at a "fast-food joint" and he rises in the nocturnal hours "to work the graveyard / shift in the linen department of a hospital" changing "the sheets on hundreds / of hospital beds . . ." But in their son's imaginative life his entire Philippine coming of age pursues him with its old potency, and the poems born of this inner turmoil shift seamlessly into a surrealistic mode in which his dreams seem more authentic than his ordinary day-to-day life in first western North America and finally in Manhattan, his new island home.

It is difficult to overestimate the daring and resourcefulness required to complete successfully this astonishingly original book. I believe this collection of poetry, so rich in the dailyness of the world and what wisdom we can draw from it, is ample evidence that Joseph O. Legaspi has arrived at a place none of his ancestors in life or in poetry have ever journeyed, and we his readers are the richer for it.

Philip Levine
June 2006

Imago

As soon as we became men
my brother and I wore skirts.
We pinched our skirt-fronts into tents
for our newly circumcised penises, the incisions
prone to stick painfully to our clothing.

I was partial to my sister's plaid skirt,
a school uniform she outgrew; my brother favored
one belonging to my grandmother, flowers
showering down his ankles.
By this stage, the skin around the tips
of our penises was swollen the size
of dwarf tomatoes.

As a cure, my mother boiled
young offshoots of guava leaves.
Behind the streamline of hung fabric,
I sat on a stool and spread
before a tin washbasin. My mother bathed
my penis with the warm broth,
the water trickling into the basin like soft rain on our roof.
She cradled my organ, dried it with cotton,
wiping off the scabs melted by the warmth,
and she wrapped it in gauze, a cocoon
around my caterpillar sex.

I then thought of the others at the verge of their manhood:
my brother to replace me on this stool,
a neighborhood of eleven-, twelve-, and thirteen-year-old
boys wearing the skirts of their sisters
and grandmothers, touched
by the hands of their mothers,

baptized by green waters,
and how by week's end
we will shed our billowy skirts,
like monarchs, and enter
the gardens of our lives.

I

Poem for My Navel

First mouth,
where my mother
first kissed
me, I offer my finger
to figure the depth
of my separation,
Gulf Divide, *terra
incognita*, crater
in the Sea of Tranquillity,
a momentary attachment,
a detachment
for the rest of my life, Pangaea
before the continental drift,
an ocean subsided into white
desert, a whirlpool
quieted, my scooped-out
heart, depression,
epicenter of my first
quake, where I heard
my father's baritone
rumbling a folk song: Mynah
Bird, in your dark light
and feathers carry
me off to a castle
made of bamboo.
        Navel: my hollowed
reminder, my dried
flower, bird's
nest, peach pit, poached
egg cup, empty
shell, scallop, my oyster
pearl-purse,

you burn along
an equator, my homeland,
my Philippines I
never conceived
of leaving, mother, dear
sustenance, my senses
in the obsidian darkness,
cross-wires of my existence
and non-existence.

Imagined Love Poem to My Mother from My Father

My mermaid, I watched you scaling milkfish.
Your hands and arms were silver,
and your body flecked
with otherworldly raindrops.
You were a silver mine to be mined.
Perched on a high branch of your mother's
mango tree, I saw only a glimmer
of the blade as you scaled the fish, up-
and-down strokes, repeatedly,
gracefully, like an artist whose gift flows
through her veins. A strand of your hair
danced across your forehead, sweat
trickled down the joyous strained lines
of your neck, and your breasts, like twin
bells, I heard their transcendental
sounds. The glistening, naked
milkfish escaped the warm Pacific
for such honor. Kismet, chosen by Neptune,
it entangled itself on the fisherman's
net and beckoned you with its fresh,
clear eyes. You sliced
its stomach, *sweet blade twisting*
in me, scooped out its innards,
the heart, pulled out the gills
from underneath its head's protective plates.
I almost fell off the tree, there was a deep
aching in my chest, and my breathing
was shallow. Crouched beside the spigot,
your brown arms pumped briskly for water
as you cleaned the fish, *cradled*
by the softest hands, blood

and scales streaming onto the earth.
Didn't you hear the fish mouthing my words
as you were salting it: *Do unto me, the spy*
up on the thick fruit tree, as you have done
unto the milkfish? One day I hope
to recite for you these verses
and in my voice you will hear,
from across the oceans surrounding
the archipelago, as if reverberated through
the ages, the voice of our future son.

The Wedding Photograph

As if it was developed by golden alchemy—
their likenesses re-created in the pulp of trees
refined to a glossy finish—
this portrait, my mother tells me, hangs
in a window of a photography studio in *Avenida*,
a market district where smokes from *jeepneys*
coil in the air for hours and women
purchase their bitter squash and pork innards.

My parents look young and full of hope.
My father is regal and handsome, his thin tie
accentuates his frame, lean as rice stalk,
not the bulge-stomached shadow that looms
over the kitchen table, later, slurping his egg yolks.
Immaculate by his side, her veil like a clump of camellias,
my mother smiles, teeth bright as promises.

The women look at this still life, and they see
the innocence of the bridal gown, the gold bands.
What they don't see is the many late nights
when my mother waited, faking interest in cross-
stitching. The fights we children witnessed
through the thin veneer of mosquito nets
like the textured matte of photographs. They did not hear
the proclamations of his hatred, the declarations
of her hatred, the slaps exchanged.

What they see is processed light, the image
trapped in paper. In front of the studio's window
these Third World wives and mothers, soot-
stained, string beans spilling out of their baskets,

cast a glimmer of recognition
while their daughters begin to dream,
praising the beauty of bride and groom
as if they are worshipping an idol.

Watermelon

1.

This morning, thirsty from the drain of night's sleep, I ate a thick slice of sweet watermelon, cold, the kind of cold that could satisfy William Carlos Williams. Forget the coffee, cream-cheesed bagel and bacon. I admit it: I'm fixated with this fruit, green outside, red on the inside, like Christmas, or my mother painted green, or like the Mexican flag without the eagle and the stripes, but with seeds, which, when sun-dried and salted, become the favorite snack food of Filipinos.

2.

I once told a tale to my younger sister of how I was conceived. Our mother went out for a walk one fine day in April, maybe June, and she walked down this path in the province, dried and brown and worn but teeming with butterflies, and the withered leaves and splinters on the ground crackled under her feet, sounding like wet wood placed on a bonfire. She walked until she stumbled upon a watermelon field where, overcome with thirst and hunger, she picked the largest, fattest fruit, cracked it open with her slender hand and found me in it. She carried me home and my true story ended. My sister rolled her ten-year-old eyes at me and said, "Mommy had sex with daddy."

3.

This summer night, I crave the satisfying sweetness of watermelon. I head to the kitchen and open the refrigerator, searching, then remembering that my father had eaten it for dinner: there is no more watermelon. All that remains is a plum, burgundy, overripe, bitten, the teeth marks I know belong to my sister.

My Grandmother, in Increments

After dinner, when the plates rest
on their rack, drying, my grandmother
ambushes me at the kitchen table.
She hands me a contract, a term
of payment for a plot of land at Rose Hills cemetery.
She asks me to calculate her leftover balance.
While I add and deduct, in long hand, she sits
there, her eyes the color of foliage
on the brink of autumn, her lips curve
as always in that wry near-smile.
Her hair was red
in her youth, born in a brown equatorial island
to Caucasian parents. It was the first thing
my grandfather noticed, she once told me.
I can still see them in the summer
of their lives, a mustachioed man with deep
tamarind eyes and his *Dancing Flame*
waltzing together, their feet gliding across the bamboo
floor which moaned like a violin.
On the table, my grandmother pinches the ripe
bananas; a gray wash of numbers waterfalls
down the page before me.
I glance at her grand hips which bore her
fifteen children, three died in infancy, my mother
in between two deaths.
In WWII, Japanese soldiers, mistaking
her for an American, confronted
my grandmother with three children in tow
and my mother inside her. It was the early phase
of the occupation, when citizens deserted the cities
for the safety of demilitarized camps
where my grandfather awaited her arrival,

where they spent weeks in a cave
that muffled the thunder of nearby war.
A soldier pulled my grandmother by her hair, threatened
her with his bayonet.
Her neck arched, she only had the sky
before her as she screamed,
Spare my babies, repeatedly in Tagalog.
That year of the war, she might as well
have given birth to me, too,
this woman who is nine-hundred-and-eighty-seven-dollars-
and-sixteen-cents away from a peaceful death.

Two Elegies

I.

Death took root at the moment of birth.
—Yukio Mishima

1.

I was far too young to know
him, the one contained in the box
layered with soft, white fabric, as if
the man was bathing, or drowning in milk.
The funeral wreaths on easels looked like artificial sunflowers.
I do not remember him being buried,
although my mother said I was there,
that tropical winter of the archipelago
when she cradled me as the earth, like the ocean, swallowed
her father, submerging him to his last baptism.

2.

As sharp as the knife was, it still crackled
the brittle shell of the century egg
when I sliced it, shell-shards all over.

Two halves: the swirling reddish yolk reminded me
of my grandfather, like an embryo, dead
in the middle. The black crystallized jelly
formed the earth where he lays buried.

3.

The *barrio* men tied the goat to a wooden fence,
a spotted, bleating kid with stumps for horns.

16

We split sapling acacia branches to feed it,
the animal chewing sideways like an old man.

The men returned and a fire was blazing nearby.
They forced a bottle of vinegar into the goat's mouth,
the beast suckling, swallowing gurgles of venom,
then another, until it was drunk, maniacal, limp.

Then the *bolo* knife plunged smoothly, penetrating
the fur, caressing the skin and throat into bloodletting.
The men hauled the dead mass over the flames,
doused it into the boiling water, lifted it, its hair
molting prematurely, as if the beast confused its seasons.

4.

I traveled here among the acacia trees to mourn the deaths:
the pigeon swallowed by a snake, the withered sunflower,
the burnt forest, the murdered goat,
the stray dog which choked on a bone,
the swan that lost its feathers,
the pearl necklace, the ivory pendant,
all the white horses,
the drowned child crossing this rapid river,
the disbeliever who slept under a mango tree, the death tree,
the disappearance of the moon, the sinking of the sun,
the hushed deaths of my misbegotten grandfathers,
and with them, charred pieces of my mother, dead,
petrified pieces of the deaths of my father, adrift.

II.

Death was a silence that gave back no answer.
—Marjorie Kinan Rawlings

When I was twelve, my father's father died
of a heart attack, a quiet passing,
he slipped away in his sleep, disturbing no one.

His funeral was a lush, three-day affair.
The open casket, in the ylang-ylang scented room,
seemed to create the orbits we voyaged.

Despite the merriment outside, the men drinking,
playing mah-jongg, the women in black laughing,
the children running along dragging a chicken by its tail,
and me, my mouth stained red sucking on salted plums,

I was drawn to the wooden coffin and my grandfather
in it, a dried seed. I rustled into the room and saw
my father before the dead. Standing by his side,
I looked up to his eyes, like two full moons.

II

The Bringers of Bread

In the prenatal, rooster-summoned morning,
my brother and I awaken and slip
through our mosquito nets as darkness
fades slowly into blue-and-bluer.

We walk into the dreamy air
not before grabbing the few *pesos* and *centavos*
waiting for us on top of our mother's bureau.

The gray road and the *click-clack* of our slippers:
we know at the end of both is the bakery.
Until then, we pounce on stray cats and birds.

We play leapfrog, leaping over each other's
bent body: bodies that evolved from the same
womb churning into one rolling animal.

At the bakery, we bask in the clean scent
of newly baked *pan de sal*, providers that we are.
We press the brown bags to our hunter's
breasts and let the warmth seep beneath our ribs.

Childhood Elegy

If our angels hover above us,
they will see a darkening cornfield, the spectral traces
of lightning bugs, and two brothers
lying among the stalks.
We come because sometimes it is hard to live.

The cornstalks, limp under the tropical sun,
revive in the cool of twilight.
The angels will know we have been here for hours.
They will land and rest their feathers around us
and whisper soothing names of winged things: *finch,*
monarch, whip-poor-will, ptarmigan, Daedalus, Icarus, Gabriel . . .

The angels will bend down and touch their faces
onto ours and borrow our eyes: *Earlier,*
a horse slipped, breaking its leg.
A boy stood beside his younger brother.
Their father came into the stable, carrying a gun.
Quails flitted out of a bamboo tree; the boy

traced the trail that had led him here,
the field tilled by the dead horse,
where his brother laid down,
dust on his cheeks.

The Sow

Her squeal pierces the silence of the Sabbath;
the resonance hangs like death
over the neighborhood.
Children run into our backyard,
collecting among patches of trampled grass to witness:
a tusked boar the color of smudged mud
riding on top of my mother's pink sow
tied to a post. She leans against a plank of the house, shrieking.
I imagine her backbone breaking at any second.
The breeders tend from the sidelines.
Occasionally they place batons under the boar's weight
to lift the swine and vary its angle on her.
Around me are children from households
where my siblings and I gather pails of leftovers
to feed to our pigs. We have seen dogs
perform similar acts. We have caught
dragonflies paired like overlapping spheres,
and as time passed, wriggling things appear in ponds.
Neighbors tack signs, and if you stroll at their gates
you'd hear the faint yelping of puppies.
Soon there will be piglets, too.
To feed and to sell.
We watch as the sow bends her front knees,
her wail as much a part of us as the morning air.

JOSEPH O. LEGASPI

Bat Hunting

Bats sharpen their fangs
on corrugated iron, and lick rust,
making their blood venomous.
If a dog dies for no reason, they are to blame.
If a rat dies, it becomes a bat in its next life.

But we are a bit older now
and know they are simply fruit-
and-insect-eating bats,
flocking in the papaya grove on the edge
of our street. And at dusk,
as the sun leaves the world to fend
for itself, we go hunting.

There are five of us, neighborhood boys
who grew up together: Eric, the oldest,
has a hint of a mustache. We stand
in the middle of the road hurling
our slippers at the flying bats,
the fingers of light
from a nearby lamp post creep at our feet.
When the birdlike shadows follow
the falling foot soles of rubber
Billy and my brother lunge at them
with cut tree branches.
This day, I throw
my slipper at the right trajectory.
The bat plummets to the ground.
We huddle around the spastic animal,
a glorified rat with its beautiful, elastic wings
like the leathery ones I imagine Satan possessed.

Suddenly my brother
stomps and the bat
squeaks. Our eyes widen.
Then Eric does the same, his foot
on the animal's head.
Billy is next. Me. Ticboy.
We go around, stomping.
Lost in a virile delusion.
Amid the shuffling of our feet,
the bat cries like my uncle's
squabs begging for food.
We stop only when the squeal
ceases to pierce the thickening darkness.
The bat's battered, head-bashed body
laid in dust. Eric drags it near
an open sewer, and kicks it in.

As it hits the murky water
we run a block to the county outpost
where our weary breathing breeds the silence
among us. We steal glances at each other,
waiting for the vengeful giant bat to arrive,
impatient for our mothers to call us to supper.
As the moon rises, a cat appears with a rat in its mouth.

Kite Season

July winds blow fiercely
in the archipelago. Boys
line themselves inside the hut,
building kites.
On bamboo floor and milking
stools, they whittle sticks,
their voices and laughter
filling the air like the dust
whirling in the equatorial noon.
Siesta, but in the hut, the boys
perfect their wooden wands,
testing the sticks' flexibility
and sturdiness by bending them
into curves. The dual sticks, shaped
in bows and arrows, are strung on paper—
lightweight, colorful onion skins,
or newspapers. Or clear plastic.
Strings are tied on the tops
and bottoms of the vertical rods.
Outside the one door,
a cauldron of melted glass
over a flame. A mound of broken
bottles next to it. The boys thrust
a few rolls of thread through
a pole, and dip them into
the thick liquid. Sands
of sharp glass cling on the strands.
Placed over discarded newspapers,
the balls of thread—silvery,
otherworldly fruits—cool themselves
underneath the shade of an acacia,
as the boys wait lazily

for the sun to move on
into the later afternoon when the wind
would still blow its sweet breath
and the war in the sky would begin.

Blood Thirst

1.

My brother and I liked to see each other bleed.
Even with towels around our fists
it took only one solid jab on the nose
to knock my brother
to the floor, blood-splattered.
My sisters and I crouched around him,
my teary-eyed brother, whimpering, ready to explode.
Upstairs, our parents were watching the 1980 U.S. presidential
election on television. Frantic, my sisters and I stuffed
a towel in his mouth, shushing him, whispering *good*
boy, good boy, reminding him of our mother's
new bamboo stick, smooth and slender.
When our parents came downstairs, we were quiet
in bed, reading, my brother, clean and sober,
and the towels soaking in detergent
by the spigot behind banana shrubs.

2.

Throughout the years, my brother and I
participated in the bloodletting.
We stepped on
broken glass, sharp stones, fish
bones. Scraped our knees on asphalt,
our wounds infected. Cut ourselves
with tin cans, fishing hooks, knives.
Were scratched by cats and thorns,
bitten by dogs.
Had our fingers burned
by firecrackers on New Year's Day, 1978.

Fought other boys cheating us at cards.
Fell down roofs and flights
of stairs, hurling our bodies
to their toughening.

3.

When he was six, a car ran over
my brother, his mangled body scraped
under the heavy machinery.

Bruised and with stitches, his right arm
and leg in casts, he had to pee
painfully in a soda bottle,
which I sometimes
held for him, smirking.

4.

The summer I was ten, my hands slipped
from husking coconuts and my face lunged
into the upright ax-blade.
Panicked, I ran and hid in a closet, my hands
touched my right cheek, the cut
so deep it was like another mouth
that can tell the story without words.
What seemed like hours later, light rushed
into the mothballed darkness. My brother stood
akimbo before the open doors, as blood
trickled down my cheek to my breast,
to my feet, damp under soaked handkerchiefs.

5.

Now, I live in New York City.
I write poetry. I work forty
hours a week, writing
for other people. On occasion
I sit through a Broadway play
while my brother tips cows
with his fraternity brothers in San Jose.
He serves chicken fingers and buffalo wings
at a pub/brewery. He beds women, some
in drunken stupor. I curl up
in bed with a cup of chamomile
and rented dirty movies,
not pushing the *play* button
until the sirens fade in the distance.

Brother

In other cultures, tribes hang the foreskin
from a branch of a fruit tree.
In ours, neighborhood boys visit
the town doctor, if they can afford him.
If not, they march to the cemetery
where a madman charges less: spread
your penis on a cement tomb and he will tear at it
with blows from a sharp stone.

Amid such folklore, my brother and I
entered manhood that summer when I was twelve, he
a year and a half younger, *Still younger*, I thought.
The one's in my favor and the half to be sure.
But I should have believed the gypsy's tea leaves
from summers past: my brother learning to ride
a bicycle after my fall; he, embracing the sea, paddling,
stroking, while brine forced itself through
my nose when I broke the waves.
These were portents: my brother
falling in love before me, driving, buying
a car and losing his virginity.

I could win only chronologically, so I was first
to spread for the doctor on his cold-horizontal,
rigid-horse of a table, my eyes
fixed to the ceiling, flinching occasionally,
quiet, flying, numbed, altered.
Done, my brother entered as I walked bowlegged
outside, resuming my rite of passage under a withering tree,
not meaning to approach the glass window.
I saw my brother lying there,
his arms curved, a pair of hollowed mountains,

31

unripe breasts, a hand over each eye
leaking tears. He was breathing prayers.
His lips tensed courageously.

The wind chimed the tree, its brown leaves
like falling bells *tink*led to the ground.
Dust lifted, there I was, leaf-kissed,
older. *A year and a half.*
There was a throbbing like a second heart
in my middle, where my body's been cut.

Shoe Box in Early Summer

When I answered the hard, abrupt knocking,
I saw a shoe box with my name written in all caps
and smudged black crayon. I picked it up, lifted
the lid and discovered a mausoleum of dead insects.
The girl who sent me this strange gift had a father
who covered their backyard porch with fly traps.
The box was sticky with flies, the dominant genus
in a multitude of cockroaches, golden honey
bees, brittle wasps of disparaging silence, stiff
grasshoppers, dragonflies, drab, burnt moths, fire
ants, the hemispherical ladybugs, maggots, daddy
longlegs and nut-bellied spiders (technically,
arachnids), fresh green-bloodied caterpillars squeezed
on her way to my door, gnats, beetles, body
pieces of deathbyhandcymbals mosquitoes,
and in the terrarium's center, a praying mantis
and a monarch, its wings' eyespot angry and condescending.

I wanted to dump the contents at her feet, the girl
with cropped hair, a slight dusting of a mustache
above her mandible lips. In the privacy
of leaves, I used to let her run her fingers
through my hair, her hands like the prayerful
forelimbs of insects. In school, however, I was continuously
cruel, my frog tongue would strike and coil around her
suffocated being. When she'd make chase with her
puckered waxy lips I'd leap and croak my disgust
and insults until she was wearied and humiliated, until shred
by shred the ribbons of her wasted dignity cluttered the school yard.

Tonight, at a wedding reception, I sit,
unaccompanied, it is early summer. Bride

and groom are posing for photographs on the verandah
against a feathery backdrop of a red sunset. Magnolias,
luminous as lightbulbs, float on the green water. And I see her
in her perpetual Catholic school uniform, hunter of insects,
wayward lover, lying sideways on a splintered floor, her eyes
swollen, on fire, as she rubs the dried mantis and dead
butterfly together for friction.

Let the dusky sun singe the couple into phosphors, let them burn.

Nocturnal

At breakfast I watched my father
devour a mackerel,
vinegar dribbling down the side
of his mouth. I watched as my mother tore
and sucked on the soft head, then spit
the skull. In our backyard, my shorts
hung from a clothesline.

Hours before, in near-light,
a sticky wad of warmth presented itself
slightly below my navel.
I tapped its phlegm consistency,
my hand formed an igloo around it.
Finally, I wiped the ooze onto my shorts
and remained uneasy until the cool, musky smear dried.

After that it occurred regularly,
and something started in me:
my hand found the inside
of my shorts whenever privately possible;
I pressed my hip harder against surfaces,
preferably wooden ones; the sight of Galapagos turtles
mating on television was enough to make me come.
Eating overripe mangoes was a joy.
I spent more time bathing.
I liked the velvety feel of house lizards,
soft as the arms of girls in my class.
Once, in school, I stole a sip of Cherry's chocolate
milk to taste her saliva on her straw.
Once, I captured a black hen and mated her
with all seven of our cock-fighting roosters
in a row, throwing her into each bamboo cage

and watching each male bird pin and mount her cackling body.
And in my sleep, I loved women
and men; I saw men love women;
a swirling bestiary, all the carnal knowledge I knew,

until sometime later, I noticed how
things fit, like God's ingenuities, or just
the way things are: the earth and sky; the pits
of avocados; lovers' entwined hands; the logic
of genitals, bees, flowers, trees and finches.
On television, I learned that swans mate
for life, like my uncle's pigeons. I remembered
one whose partner was eaten by a rat, and she did not
mate again. Outside of school, I daydreamed
as much about Cherry's giggle as the tiny hairs
that ran down the back of her neck.
And when I witnessed my father
kissing my mother, gently,
on the lips,
I realized that I belong
to a stricter realm of the senses.
What did I know? What have I to say
of the savagery and tenderness of love?

III

Sleeping Together

Inside mosquito netting, my father and I sleep
on the same mat, the soft, crucifix weave
of *buri* leaves, laid out on the floor
between two beds. My sisters, tangled
in floral sheet, occupy the bed on the right,
Jeniffer, all wispy brown hair and cream-
colored skin, Jayne, square-jawed
with hair like deep archipelago nights.
My mother—the mare-beauty of her—sleeps
on the other bed with her newborn daughter
suckling at her breast, beside her, my brother,
abysmal in the process of his weaning.
I am seven, occupying that privileged space
beside my father, life and life-giver. Lights
burn all the while. Moths' wings collect
onto the net. The room swirls
with breathing, a son's world unfolding.

The Circumcision

Light diffused through the blanket. I faced the rise
and fall of my father's stomach and plunged my hand carefully through
the elastic waistband of his shorts,
startled at how different his penis
looked from mine: darker, not only the skin
but the hair around it like tree shadows.
Its head, a gravity-defying, moth-eating house lizard,
had no flap of skin over it. How free it looked,
powerful, shaped like a bullet, and instead of taking life,
it gave life. I petted it. My father
shifted to my direction and continued his snoring. Slowly,
the penis rose as if it was absorbing the light, the air,
my touch. It stiffened, flaunting itself
as the center of the universe.
I wanted my penis to be
like my father's, the union of beauty and purpose,
and five years later, on a thirsty July afternoon,
he asked me and my brother to *hurry up*,
he was taking us to the doctor for our circumcisions.
I buttoned my pants cautiously as my sisters teased:
They are sending you both to the butcher.
My mother stood on the threshold
and sent us on our way, the most important men
in her life, her father many years dead. I held my father's
hand, all two blocks to the clinic
where I spread for the doctor, and thanked the inventor
of anesthesia. I heard the snipping sound vividly, felt
the smooth trickle of warm blood and the otherworldly
contact of hard metal on skin. The relief of the operation's
end was ephemeral. My penis resembled little of my father's:
the flap removed, the head smooth and tender, yet
it looked ragged, humbled, beaten, like a man down on his luck.

When the anesthesia wore off, the throbbing pain
seemed to be eating up my groin. My brother and I
inched our way back home,
our smiling father walking patiently beside us.
How funny we must be to him,
his minions bowlegged with what might as well have been
egg shells in between our thighs. When the stitches
heal, I thought, and when the raw skin has time
to acclimate to the elements—air, touch—I will possess
the potential. My father placed a hand on each of our shoulders,
and there in the doorway, as if a painting in its gilded frame,
was my mother waiting for her sons.

The Scheme of Beauty

Father, I stand beside you, in the mirror,
staring at your reflection primping,
putting on pomade
that smells like manufactured mint.
I comb in the green gel, too.
My hair glistens in the oily,
plowed blackness.

Of your two sons,
I look more like you,
everyone says so,
like the split sides of a coconut.
In me they see you in your youth again,
except I don't have the Spanish red
highlights of your hair,
your clear skin, the masculine
lilt of your hips.
You were far more handsome than I.

From the town elders I learned
you were the most eligible bachelor
in the county of San Ysidro:
firm, confident body; a good smoker—*can
maintain the habit without retaining the smell*—
an office job in the city.
They said your mother ate nothing
but white corn during her pregnancy.

My mother with her sisters used to wait for you
at dusk when you, in your madras shirt,
after work, would pass outside their window.
When you approached her confidently, she leaned

on the sill, her hair flowing like dark river over her shoulder
and her face inflamed by the glow of a Christmas lantern.

And your life has brought us here: squared in the mirror,
a matter both solid and liquid, a portrait of father and son,
your clothes always matching down to your socks,
your lapels spreading like birds' wings.
You would then rush out-of-doors to work
and I would not see you again
until the morning when
you face that mirror
and I join you in recognition
of myself, of this whole scheme of beauty,
of the time when I admire you.
I would scoop a teaspoonful of pomade
between my fingers and eat it.

Desert Postcards

1.

Before I knew it his plane hovered then passed above me,
leaving a trail of sonic reverberations demonstrating
my grade school lesson on Doppler effect.
That was the first of my father's three-year absence to Saudi Arabia
where he worked at oil refineries, bringing fossils back to life.

I stood there, insignificant, bursting
with awe, my neck arched like an inverted *u*
as the sky dimmed, darkening the grease-stained airport floor.

2.

On my tenth, eleventh and twelfth birthdays
the mailman came
shoving mail down our mailbox—
a choking throat—
where each year a 3-D Disney postcard stuck out
like a tongue.

When shifted by angles and degrees, light animated
the images trapped in layers of prismatic paper:
Pinocchio flies into the arms of *Geppetto*;
Bambi grazes then looks up the antlered hill;
Hanzel and *Gretel* skip down the path, golden
and green, to the gingerbread house.
These orphans, these orphaned children,
I know why they're happy lost in the woods.

Typhoon

The windows and doors are boarded.
From outside, the furious typhoon bangs
and rattles like my drunken father locked out of the house.
Inside, my brother and sisters join me around the campfire
of candles. The typhoon toppled an electrical post.
It howls. It hurls matter into matter. We hear
the thrashing flight of sheet iron, the crack
of branches splitting from the trees.
The house shakes, and we huddle
in the neardarkness, as if
cowering back into the primitive.
We share stories while bending near the candles,
collecting the stalactites of wax
we'd later feed to the flames.
We talk about the neighborhood children,
earlier covering the ground with chalk-drawings
of suns, birds caught between two skies. The rain
fell anyway, the suns vanished in the downpour.
My sister tells us about orphans in nunneries,
so underfed they eat worms, bathed
so infrequently that truffles grow between their toes
and pigs follow them wherever they go.
And we remember a lake in the province, hidden
by woodland in the east, opposite high rocks
from where we dove into the ethereal silence of the water.
Then a sudden crash reverberates from the house's swollen
blackness, distinct from the storm. It continues for some
time, not without trying to stifle itself like a whisper. I call for my parents,
though unknown to me, in that dark chamber of the house
while the world outside is seemingly coming to an end.

Fetching My Father

How did we get here? My father sprawled on the bed, sleeping,
        dried remnant
of his retching on the side of his mouth. I take off his shirt, pants,
        socks, my father
a pink newborn with every clothing shed. Calm as a napping infant.
        I wipe
his face with a damp towel, banishing the offending stain, traveling
        over the slopes
of his eyes, *my eyes*, the hill of his nose, *my sisters'*, and the thinning
        hayfield
of his head. In the sky, the equatorial moon, the largest, brightest
        moon, bears
witness, its light streaming through the window like angels' dresses.
        It is a satellite,
I learned that in school last week, this non-light weaver, a massive
        rock of a reflector,
harnesses light from the sun. Should I give up on the moon? I curl
        up next to my father,
I am a seahorse, a nautilus, I am the ear's cochlea, and again wait for
        sleep.

Earlier, the neighbors down the block slaughtered a goat.
The killing commemorated the first birthday of the household's
        youngest son,
the preparations spilling over to festivities, which boiled over like a
        witch's cauldron
onto the street. At dusk, strings of electric lights appeared overhead
        like fireflies,
illuminating the women fanning themselves, and the throng of
        crimson-faced men,
my father among them, gathered around a long table, gambling and
        drinking, the air
filled with their boisterous joy. Young boys circled hungrily, sons

and brothers,
remoras wishing themselves into sharks or ships. It was a lucrative
     venture:
the grown-ups loose with their *pesos* when they asked the boys to make
     storeruns
for cigarettes, matches, salted cashews. And the men raged with their
     merriment
into the deepening night as the boys, one by one, fell to their lupine
     slumber.

Sometime after midnight, I was awakened by my mother, rocking my
     shoulders.
Please fetch your father, she said, and I walked the empty street leading
     to him,
my singing, argumentative father. I tugged at his arm, his shirt,
     mumbled my coaxing;
he shooed me away like a fly; lifted me by my underarms and stood me
     on the corner,
promising he would go home with me after one last drink. Nearby,
     the goat's skull,
picked clean, wan as the moon, dangled from a tall fence post, dogs curled
     underneath it.
Standing up, I drifted in and out of sleep. This was only the beginning:
     sometimes
my mother will be with me, sometimes I will go alone, and when my
     brother is older
he will accompany me, as he will when I buy warm bread in the morning.
When we walked home that first night, my father slung his arm around
     the wing span
of my back, and I felt his weight on me, dented by the gravity of his
     intoxication,
his vulnerability, his loneliness, as we wobbled down the road. In
     the darkness,
I heard the songs of night birds, crickets, frogs, stray cats and dogs,
     my song.

The Eye of the Wound

After her concoction of guava leaves, ginger and sorghum has boiled
and simmered, wafting ghostly, ethereal smoke, my mother,
in treating my wound, places the slender knife she uses for gutting
small fishes over the burner. I sit on a chair in our kitchen, smelling
of heated steel, smoked milkfish and grease, my older sister stands
behind me. Last week, running from a mob of boys in an exhilarating
        game
of tag, I tumbled and scraped against the macadam: asphalt, pebbles, tar,
        glass
crystals, bits of bones burrowed in my knee. Now the wound is infected,
        inflamed,
swollen, and when I'd bend my knee, pustules would erupt, breaking
        through the scabs,
like tectonic plates, releasing creamy pus, at times, swirled with blood.
My mother must excavate the eye of the wound.
First, she cleanses my injury with her broth, a warm comfort, the liquid
trickling into a tiny corrugated iron basin. Then she tells me to close my
        eyes.
My sister's arms, crisscrossed against my chest like parachute straps,
        brace
themselves, holding me down to the chair as I jerk from the knife's
        searing entry.
As it pierced through my left knee, just above the skull of the patella, I
        feel a burst
of thick fluid running slowly down my leg, then, the digging, thin steel
        roving inside me,
my mother a miner in search of ore, and for what seems like an eternal
        age of mercy,
she pulls out the knife, lifting it up to show me a pearl-sized clot of
        blood, glistening
like the rich, dark red of petroleum. I wipe my sodden eyes; my sister
        unbuckles

her arms and proceeds to wash my lower leg with my mother's brew.
     The burning
is subsiding, fire combating fire, the pain throbbing in distant waves.
     Through
the years, I will be healed and saved by women, again and again, but
     despite this,
the body will seek its lost passion, evade the sex that seared its flesh,
     the body never forgets.

Killing a Chicken

My mother killed chickens
making the same crisp sound
of separation: a guava from its stem,
a fowl's breakage from its life.

I liked chickens enough; I respected them.
My roosters had names: *Kukoro, Loro, Talisayin.*
But my romance with them was a detachable bridge.
When served to us fried, garnished in garlic,
or in stew, my siblings and I would exclaim
how tasty *Kukoro* was!

Weeks after my ninth birthday, while feeding
the chickens worms I gathered from a ditch,
my uncle's shadow engulfed me, his hand
rubbed my hair as he entered the coop in a gust
of feathers and dust. He brought out a plain
white hen, one unnamed because she was unappealing,
too common in her whiteness—a finch, a gecko.
I followed my uncle to the cold cement steps.
Sitting down, he tucked the chicken between
his thighs, its head drawn back, neck exposed
for plucking. Nearby: a pot full of water
over burning firewood, a pear-shaped bowl.
My uncle smiled, his hand beckoned me to him.
He handed me a razor, the kind for shaving. I took it.
He presented me with the tender, plucked neck.
My hand like steel. I rocked back and forth.
The razor sliced smoothly,
with sincere grace.

The hen quivered, but it was not her life
I was thinking of, but my mother's:
the life she had given up for her children,
the many deaths she performed, the hearts
and gizzards she had eaten. The liver. It is harder
for a mother, a giver of life, one
who carries an egg-filled nest in her body,
to take a life as I had done with ease,
the fire crackling behind me, the razor
as warm in my hand as the blood
trickling into the bowl.

Faith Healer

Penetrating the surrounding trees, my mother and I march
to a *nipa*-hut temple in a clearing. We join a line
of people, mostly from distant villages, waiting to see
the faith healer. The new moon settles herself in the sky. Hens
perch on invisible branches. We come to cure my asthma.
By age ten, I have exhausted doctor-prescribed relief.

Inside the hut, the faith healer, a dried leaf
of a man, a green bandanna knotted in front of his head,
asks me to undress. Crucifixes on claustrophobic walls,
a shrine of idols and palms unfolds in a corner.

I climb on the bamboo table.
The night deepens. My mother sits
by a window, framed by darkness.
The old man stands over me. He drenches
his hands with oil—the pungent smells of coconut
and anise—rubs my front, swirls his slippery hands
on my chest, then rolls me over, his thumbs press
the central vertebrae on my neck, electric,
his wrinkled hands roam, my skin glistens
to my toes, while the man chants
not exactly words, but a song,
both joyful and difficult.

He gives me a glass of white fluid
with menthol and aniseed. It drifts
down my throat like warm whole milk.
My mother helps me with my clothes,
this woman present as always,
every time I was bedridden, frightened,
or coughing fitfully. With me when I was weak-

kneed and breathless on a curb after a half-block's run.
With me on the sidelines watching other children play.

After giving the healer
a contribution, my mother takes my hand
and we saunter past the string
of people, obedient sheep in the gloom,
past where the light
from the hut is faint,
past the moon-haunted forest,
to where the clearing is swallowed by trees.

Ode to My Mother's Hair

The provincial
river is transformed,
my mother
in a clear-sky afternoon
washes her hair,
dark as cuttlefish ink.
Between
her flat palms,
she rubs it
with silt, twisting
the strands
as if starting a fire:

my mother's Promethean
crown of smoke, daughter
of a woman with hair like fire.

I have seen photographs:
my mother pony-tailed
as a girl, split-
ends, braided,
molasses stuck
and formed
prickly discs
like coiled, poisonous caterpillars;
like blackholed flowers
in her follicle garden;
tangled little
mushrooms.

As a child
in the fringes of sleep,

when my fill of colostrum
swirled warmly inside me,
I often burrowed
my mole face
in my mother's hair,
the darkness beyond the banana grove.
I remember
how it brushed against my eyelids,
fending off the midnight dogs
of sleeplessness; tickled
my ears, deadening
the skeletons
of nightmares;
and how I breathed in
strands, which planted
the seed of the tree of memory.

My mother's hair is domestic hair:
absorbent to the scent
of her cooking—
milkfish, garlic, goat;
her fur of sweeping dust
clipped
in a bun, with wisps
that dangle
on her face, and dance
to floor scrubbing by coconut husk
to laundry five children soiled
to my father's pulling and shaking.

When my youngest sister
was born, our mother chopped
her hair, the incubating black hen
of her head ousted the starlings.
In hope of a reparation

for what we had driven her to do
I gathered locks
from her brush,
tied them with blue ribbon
and buried them in our backyard,
dusting the plot
with sugar and cocoa,
moistening the mound with honey—
all the goodness from the world of the living.
I believed
the earth resurrects
what is nourished in its belly.

And in this river,
my mother's wet, swirling hair
reminds me
of monsoon seasons
when our house,
besieged by wind and water,
teetered and threatened to split open,
exposing the diorama
of our barely protected lives
with my mother, seated, telling stories
to her children collected around her
while my sister and I are brushing her mane,
smelling of rose soap,
sprouting by candle light,
her hair which is always the other half of the world.

IV

Departure: July 30, 1984

We were not prepared for it—
America, the land cut like a massive slab
of steak. Our mother did not sit us down
to explain, and nothing was said
over the black coffee and rice
soup at mealtimes. My siblings and I approached
our inevitable leaving with numb
acceptance, as people do under martial law.

Days prior to the date, things disappeared
in the house: the display cabinet taken away by an aunt,
the wedding gift china wares in it sold, except for the blue plates
and swan-shaped bowls that would not survive the journey.
The rice bin was given to a family friend; knives
to Uncle Leo; school uniforms, cousins; roosters divided
among the men; floral fabrics for the women; dried
mangoes and stale squid candies for the neighborhood
children; a twin bed transported upstairs
for my sister staying to complete college.

That late July morning, the *jeepney* arrived,
as hired, the sun held dominion over the blinding sky,
a zephyr funneled through the narrowing streets
of Manila. The steady procession of
well-wishers in our house did not halt,
my father handing out *pesos*
as if he was paying for our safe passage.
Surrounded by luggage and boxes huge
as baby elephants, we were each given
a dollar bill, our firsts, as the *jeepney* drove off
to take us to the airport, leaving behind a throng
of onlookers waving violently, and a tearful, older sister

who, years later, would reenact this disappearing act,
this fading scene of a rooster-lined road of this
cockfighting, banana tree-lush town speeding away,
lost in the kinetic gray cement and dark smoke of exhaust.

The Immigrants' Son

In my house, nuzzled in leafy suburbia,
ants nest on the china ware and chip away
the designs; seafood remains frost-bitten
in the freezer; pubic hair thrives under the dampness
of mats and towels; and my grandmother's overripe
bitter squashes burst in the backyard,
dropping to the ground, uneaten.

I give you my mother,
mourning our adulthood
like any other deaths.
She holds nightly vigils
watching shows she doesn't care for.
Forget it. She has given up on prayers;
she doesn't read books. She worries
about her sons chasing white women,
about her daughters being chased
by white men, or worse, black men.
My mother misses the splintered Old World
house where my grandmother resided
upstairs with her unmarried children
and in the apartment rooms below lived
her married children and their children,
families sleeping side by side
on beds pushed together.

And I give you a memory
of that year when my aunt gave birth
to her firstborn: twin stillbirth boys,
grayish, mummified cupids.
They were placed in a pickled egg jar
and buried in the dark, musty earth

beneath our protruding house,
creaking heavily under too much weight.

Looking out at the backyard, leaning
against a weakened wall, a splinter
throbbing in the palm of my hand, I wonder
whether I would find the jar half-filled with
brittle baby bones
if I dug deep enough where
the next overripe bitter squash falls.

Alaska

That summer back in the desert,
I had grown too big for my family.
In that two-bedroom apartment
which squeezed seven adults
I was one more stone
thrown in a jar filled to the brim
with water. My college books spilled
out of closets, my pine cone collection piled
up between intersections of furniture,
and my clothes baked in their trunk.
Nights, I slept on the couch,
often dreaming of birds
and skeletons, skeletal
angels, as my brother turned
his heavy, comatose body
on an air mattress
below me. That summer
I spent hours cramped
in the bathroom, reading, just
me, Kierkegaard, Faulkner
and Gide. Life traveled
like a boat
in the middle of a lake.
My mother talked slowly,
my sisters dressed slowly,
the ceiling was too low,
too little room to visit.
And I was tired of the same
reel of scenes,
of the women gathered
around the table, cutting
bok choy and tripe,

my father asleep, to be
awakened and driven
to work at 10:30 p.m. and me,
slumped on the couch, watching
a documentary on Alaska,
the final frontier
of dogsleds, Eskimos,
and big chunks of ice
splitting away from glaciers,
crashing into the frigid ocean.

The Red Sweater

slides down into my body, soft
lambs wool, what everybody
in school is wearing, and for me
to have it my mother worked twenty
hours at the fast-food joint.
The sweater fits like a lover,
sleeves snug, thin on the waist.
As I run my fingers through the knit,
I see my mother over the hot oil in the fryers
dipping a strainer full of stringed potatoes.
In a twenty-hour period my mother waits
on hundreds of customers: she pushes
each order under ninety seconds, slaps
the refried beans she mashed during prep time,
the lull before rush hour, onto steamed tortillas,
the room's pressing heat melting her makeup.
Every clean strand of weave becomes a question.
How many burritos can one make in a continuous day?
How many pounds of onions, lettuce and tomatoes
pass through the slicer? How do her wrists
sustain the scraping, lifting and flipping
of meat patties?   And twenty

hours are merely links
in the chain of days startlingly similar,
that begin in the blue morning with my mother
putting on her polyester uniform, which,
even when it's newly-washed, smells
of mashed beans and cooked ground beef.

My Father in the Night

My father sleeps when the city rages
around him and rises to work the graveyard
shift in the linen department of a hospital.
Boxed in his heavy-curtained room,
the glass window shut,
we would think him dead if not for his
snoring, amplified by the thick, stagnant air
which holds the sound before it
dissipates and is absorbed by the walls.
Before he leaves for work,
my father sits at the table, eating
his meat and rice, his children
bewildered by the sight of him.
With boiled eggs and bread slices in a brown bag,
he steals away into the urban darkness
while his wife stumbles into bed, alone,
rearranging the disheveled sheets.
            And my father in the night
changes the sheets on hundreds
of hospital beds, the kind where he laid
when his skin was like potato-sack burlap
from dialysis and chemotherapy.
He removes the soiled pillow cases, replacing
them with starched ones.   He puts on the white
sheet, unfolding it in the air like a woman's
skirt, settling it down onto the mattress.

The Socks

This pair once belonged to my father,
army green,

golden on the thinning
heels and toes, decades old—

they have disappeared into the dryer-netherworld
only to return repeatedly, wiser than before—

their elastics still grasp my lower calves.
When I slip into them,

I see my father in his footwear, like Mercury,
a copper-eyed young man, like myself,

brewing with stormy promise,
prepared to soar over the dusty world.

Dear socks, don't lead me astray.
Propel me from this dissatisfied life

to places where my father has never been.

Men with Breasts

When I see men with breasts,
mammillary, twin elfin mounds
bulging through
shirts, I suppress
the bubbles of emotions
that might burp out of me—a moan,
a giggle. I think: nubile children trapped
in adult men, daughters
hidden in their bodies,
the women in these men
manifesting themselves.
Do their hands make pilgrimages
to these holy places? Do they
gently stroke the knobs
of their areolas to summon
a lover from anywhere across snowbanks or Eden fields?
Or do they curse them
for obstructing intimate embrace
with pillows? Do they desire
the armor chests of Greek
heroes, demigods and gods?
At the beach they parade
in front of me like platters
of fruits: Chinese plums,
glossy pink and cup-sized, pale
strawberries, hairy kiwis. My father,
too, possesses a pair of dwarf papayas,
elongated, sagging into cusps
of rosy resin, languid, nestled
on his stomach like the Buddha's.
I know my father's breasts
are empty and my thirst

will remain
unquenched, I can suck
and suckle, work them
like the teats of a newly birthed sow
or bitch, play the spherical
instrument of his nipples
with my tongue to hear
celestial music, and there will be no
warm, nourishing colostrum.

This Face

Eyes like magpies in milk,
the caves of the nose, lips
the darker petals of pink roses;
it is a face of an Asian
derived from the Malays, the hunters in Java, the Chinese
cooling themselves in the banks of the Yangtze,
it is my father's face.

Asian men: in America it could be
another word for mule,
the sterile,
almost female,
the *gook, nips*, and *flips*
who cook beautiful meals with bean sprouts,
cashews and water chestnuts;
who slice their meats in slivers;
who eat food with sticks like slender fingers;
who do laundry for a living;
who are passive;
who are more cerebral than sexual;
who are prisoners of their genetics:
the undersized, soft frame, almost hairless bodies,
the Mongoloid features.

I see the face that looks back at me:
the porcupined eyebrows,
the furrows of the forehead,
the overbite. Same as when I hunch
over a basin of water,
as when I close my eyes to sleep—
it is the face of someone

who is the source of my conceit, my Asian-ness,
my maleness. It is my father's
and I love it.

JOSEPH O. LEGASPI

Visiting the *Manongs* in a Convalescent Home in Delano

Those mountains, ocher in the distance,
resemble the wrinkled skins
of the *manongs* from Delano,
a town north of Bakersfield that smells
like the first rain after a drought, the pungent
collision of earth-dryness and sky-wetness.

The fields near the highways are packed
with rows upon rows of sweet melons and sprouts.
Filipino migrant workers picked them
for cents: winter peas, oranges, bushels of apples.
Their backs arched like bent bamboos.

Santa Maria. Barstow. Salinas.
Fresno. Seattle. Juneau.
The west is too familiar
to these lonely old men trapped in their rooms
filled with photographs of white girls
they had loved but cannot marry.
Each told the story of the collective,
the many eyes of a single pineapple:
I came to America at sixteen, at fourteen,
at twelve, aboard a dysenteried ship . . .

Looking at the east, shunned by the west,
they wander as ghosts in-between worlds, haunting,
and yet haunted by their own ghosts,
the white membranes over their eyes like sadness.
This is all we know, said the *manongs,*
To harvest grapes, you must destroy the vines.

California Beaches

A dead infant was washed ashore on a beach in California.
The next day, another stillborn was found
thrown up by the sea
some shoreline miles away. Both
had their umbilical cords like snakes
eating at their entrails.

People who stared at the red glow of dusk
believed them to be signs of the apocalypse.
They went to the beaches and lit candles on the sand.
Lovers stayed away from the shores.
Men grew more suspicious of women.
Fathers imagined what their offspring would become.
Mothers chose longer books to read to their children.

Night after night, I dreamt:
A meteor struck and I walked among the ruins,
ashes, and cracked granite. I came across
moving, infested water that lead to a cesspool,
and afloat was a mummified, stillborn child,
skeletal, blue-black, eyes
closed. It had its thumb in its mouth,
a marble-sized opening.
I lifted the child, held it to the warmth
of my chest, and as if it was alive,
I whispered to it, "Hush little darling, don't you cry . . ."

When I awaken, parched and made suddenly dumb
by the forgotten darkness, I remember them,
my cousins, twin, premature boys
born dead from their mother.
They were so tiny they fit in a pickled egg jar

and were buried under our house
in a country surrounded
by water, which I left years ago.
They have come searching for me.

First Cigarette

When I remember that first cigarette—
Hope (its brand name), paper ivory
between my thieving fingers, pilfered
from a pocket of my father's lifeless
long-sleeve shirt, a scarecrow hung
over a chair—the scene unfolds in astral
projection. I see the top of a child's
head, a nest of disheveled fur, his jittery
legs like frogs' legs on the rim of the toilet bowl.
Striking a match, he creates fire
and lights a cigarette, which, to him,
is brittle bone, jeweled embers,
something he could breathe in
to fill his young body, something
like passion, courage, class.
Without coughing, he savors the warm
whirlpool in his chest, the tickling of menthol
in his throat and the eruption of fumes
from his fish mouth.
He will draw upon this comfort
during the initial chapters of his future life
in new cities—Manila, Los Angeles,
London, New York—where he is foreign,
and the foreign is strange. In time
immemorial, the boy hides behind the moss-
green stall with its paint peeling, and the late
morning light slants harshly from the high window
while smoke rises like a soul vacating a body.

Little Blackbird

Up on a tree across the yard, a raven thrashes,
showering the ground with pine needle rain.
You jolt in delight, speak
your baby-gurgle, point your pale
caterpillar finger at that dark commotion
not unlike a feathery stirring of memories.
In my nesting arms, I carry you as my father perhaps
once carried me and how I've seen
your father hold you, blood
of my blood, my sister's daughter.
                              I have been gone too long,
traveled distances I myself sometimes cannot bear,
but the sweetness of the first words
and raven sounds which roll from your tongue
has made me remember what I left behind:
somewhere in a timeless place
a boy rides a horse through rice puddles
a boy feeds on the ivory meat of coconuts
a boy suckles on the udders of a carabao
and under a tropical twilight dome fireflies scatter like stars
onto a field where that same boy falls into a deep, silent slumber.
Now, you sleep, little blackbird.
I will chase away the cat, destroyer
of the moth of dreams,
and when you awaken
you will again restore my sight to the threads that bind.

Three Muses

I. The Teacher, *for Sharon Olds*

Her tram, a red gift-wrapped box, descended
from the sky. Sitting on a bench,
on this island, I had watched the mechanical sedan—
the calculated movements of an automaton—
as it wedged itself into the landing station
and let her out. My back to her, I sense her walking past
me on the road a tree shadow away, the right, left,
right of her feet on the corner of my eye. I swerve
for scrutiny. She wears a white blouse—not immaculate,
like her hair, ashened by grays—and a green skirt waving towards
the river, a barge plowing through it like a tractor on a field of spinach.
She looks at the water, hesitates, pulls forward, then
back, cranes her watch to her glasses. She walks
along the embankment, weak to the water's allure,
her pace unhurried, calm in its contentment.
Stopping momentarily, she gazes across the East River,
at the skyscrapers of Manhattan, breathing in everything.
Her skirt rides stiffly on her waist, she resumes
her progress, an atom in the landscape.

II. The Sister

When her door was left ajar,
I peeked at the vertical slit, finding my sister
horizontal on her bed, writing. It made
me think of the cross; I knew
somehow what I was doing was wrong.
The intrigue was too much to bear
and I promised to think angelic thoughts
the rest of each of those days.

Sometimes I only saw her legs dangling
in the air like ducks; sometimes,
her curved back, a new woman's body,
lithesome in its blossoming, yet boyish and hard;
and framed by the wooden wall and door,
her face, never had I seen her ethereal except during those times.

One day, when my sister was not home
and the boredom of the afternoon settled in like dust
on a peach, I sneaked into her room, dug
through her drawers, and unearthed
the journal, red, unadorned, inconspicuous.
I dove onto her bed, flipping through pages
of poetry, love poems
she had written, one
insipid poem after another,
all achingly sweet.
First, a chuckle escaped from my lips,
a covey of sparrows,
then a guffaw, a murder of crows.
Suddenly, I turned and saw her,
in tears, standing at the half-open door
where I usually crouched.

III. The Mother

She took away the crayons and washed
the walls until they were white again.
My mother gave me old newspapers to play with.
My hands itched. I tore
at the gray papers, first, in anger, forming
undefined shapes, later, in increasing amusement,
more intricate two-dimensional figures—
the world taken out of the walls.

For years then I drew out of the rectangles the contours
of elephants, carabaos and people.
I ripped a herd of Appaloosas;
tended to the lacerated bodies of my soldiers;
shredded rain for my reenactment of Noah's ark.
On the end of each paper-cutting day, my mother
collected the discarded pieces of newspaper
and wiped my hands and face,
tenderly, with a warm towel.
What was she washing away from my skin?
One afternoon, the smudged towel hung
from a chair and I looked at my right hand.
On my thumb, a toppled *a*, a trapped snail;
a splinter of an *i*; a fading *k*.
On my other fingers, the *b*, *d* and *p* assembled
like musical notes; the hairs on the *o*;
the conjunction *ng*, a bridge.
I licked my thumb, pressed it on the wall,
and the *a* stayed. Twice more
until I spelled *ako*: me, in Tagalog.
I turned around and saw my mother,
her hands on her waist.
She left the room, returning with a pencil and a notebook—
clean, lined paper—and we sat down,
my mother showing me the way
as I rest my thumb on the pencil buttressed
by my finger where a corn will bloom.

§§§

Sleep

There are horses galloping.
Skeletons rattle their bones beneath the dirt.

I eat lamb for breakfast
and the ewes inside me lament.

Half moons are caught in my fingernails.

When the horses come they bring the road with them.
I stand
here, a dark valley.

The pigs squeal in forked tongues.

A figure approaches;
he has the lights of my fingernails to guide him.
My grandfather. My mother's father,
the first to cease the world
as soon as I entered it.

He walks by, so close
the hairs of my arms brush his.

The roosters roar, laying their eggs.

Others follow: grandmother, aunts, cousins, uncles, grandfather.
I wait for the secrets of the dead to drip out of their mouths,
I wait to ride the fiery, galloping horses.

CavanKerry's Mission

Through publishing and programming, CavanKerry Press connects
communities of writers with communities of readers. We publish
poetry that reaches from the page to include the reader, by the finest
new and established contemporary writers. Our programming brings
our books and our poets to people where they live, cultivating new
audiences and nourishing established ones.

Other Books in the New Voices Series

Howard Levy, *A Day This Lit*
Karen Chase, *Kazimierz Square*
Peggy Penn, *So Close*
Sondra Gash, *Silk Elegy*
Sherry Fairchok, *Palace of Ashes*
Elizabeth Hutner, *Life with Sam*
Joan Cusack Handler, *GlOrious*
Eloise Bruce, *Rattle*
Celia Bland, *Soft Box*
Catherine Doty, *Momentum*
Georgianna Orsini, *Imperfect Lover*
Christopher Matthews, *Eye Level, 50 Histories*
Joan Seliger Sidney, *Body of Diminishing Motion*
Christian Barter, *The Singers I Prefer*
Laurie Lamon, *The Fork Without Hunger*
Robert Seder, *To the Marrow*
Andrea Carter Brown, *The Disheveled Bed*
Richard Jeffrey Newman, *The Silence of Men*
Ross Gay, *Against Which*